Henry M. Hyndman

Commercial Crises of the Nineteenth Century

Henry M. Hyndman

Commercial Crises of the Nineteenth Century

ISBN/EAN: 9783337378417

Printed in Europe, USA, Canada, Australia, Japan

Cover: Foto ©Suzi / pixelio.de

More available books at **www.hansebooks.com**

Commercial Crises

A Discussion of
The Present Economic Situation
and the Origin of Crises

BY

I. H. LIONBERGER, CHAIRMAN

OF

The American Credit-Indemnity Company

Published by
The American Credit-Indemnity Company.

Copies to be had on application.

St. Louis, 1920.

INDEX.

PREFACE.

In a series of essays I have attempted to explain various interesting aspects of economic problems which are apt to be ignored. All of them involve nearly identical considerations, and as each was intended to be complete in itself, repetition was inevitable. In former essays I discussed the Meaning of Business, the Meaning of Property, and Inflation and Prosperity.

This essay is an attempt to show why crises are inevitable wherever business is conducted with borrowed money. A crisis is caused in my opinion by inefficient pro-

duction, an increase in the cost of
goods, rising prices, the stress of
the high cost of living upon people
of narrow incomes, a lessening demand for goods at such prices,
over-production of costly goods,
falling prices and the inability of
the merchant under such circumstances to pay his debts with available resources.

I have tried to establish this
theory by showing what caused or
precipitated other crises, and discussing the various influences now
obvious which should, if the theory
be correct, tend to cause a crisis
in the future; and also to suggest
what precautions should now be
taken to mitigate such a calamity.

I. H. L.

January, 1920.

CRISES.

PART I.

Introductory. — A cursory examination of the history of America will discover that every generation of men has had to confront two or three commercial crises of greater or less severity. If we seek for the causes of such disturbances, we shall find as many explanations as crises; this one having been attributed to paper money, that one to extravagance, another to the strain of competition, or over-production, or a collapse of credit, etc. So various are the causes assigned that our perplexity is increased rather than diminished by investigation. We perceive a startling similarity between all such convulsions, but can not find any definite, persistent influence to which all of them may be attributed.

 Periods of active trade ending abruptly in shocking disaster have been followed by years of lassitude and dullness; yet in the hour of darkest gloom symptoms of recovery have become evident, and by slow degrees prosperity has been re-established. Prosperity seems always to have been fraught with disaster, and times of adversity seem always to have been fruitful of good. There were nine crises between 1800 and 1900, and two between 1900 and 1919. Why does the same thing happen over and over again; what is the explanation of what seem to be the fixed habits of business?

The explanations to which I have referred are not only conflicting but unsatisfactory. Paper money can not have caused all panics. There was no inflation between 1900 and 1907. Moreover, the immediate effect of inflation is to stimulate business in a very remarkable way. Too much paper money or too much bank credit is dangerous, but why is it put out? Why do men sometimes borrow more than they can pay, and why does credit result in loss sometimes and not always?

Waste or extravagance is a relative term. What is a proper expenditure for one man is extravagance for another. Expenditure within one's means is not extravagance. Moreover, where people practice economy or self-denial trade languishes and wages fall. If spending be the life of trade, how can extravagance lead to disaster, unless it be excessive in the sense that it involves an expenditure which overruns the productive capacity of the people? That it does not do so is evident if we remember that every crisis seems to be characterized by what is called over-production.

Speculation is an incident of progress and the effect of enterprise. It fails because the prosperity upon which it relies comes to an abrupt and unexpected end. Like extravagance, it seems to be rather the forerunner than the cause of a collapse in industry. During a period of prosperity incomes increase rapidly, and some part is spent and some part invested. No harm should result, save to the spenders. Why should legitimate trade be suddenly arrested by speculation; why should all incomes be suddenly reduced? To say that competition kills business is to contradict the maxim that it is the life of trade.

None of these suggestions is quite satisfactory; none explains all crises. Yet we find persuasive proof in the sequence and similarity of events that precede all of them that substantially identical influences are always operating. Business is dull, then improves, then is active, then excited, and then it collapses.

The sequence of these events suggests a plausible conjecture: business is dull because men practice self-denial and the distribution of goods is arrested; it improves after a period of saving; becomes active as men spend more freely; so remains until extravagance shall have overrun resources; and then collapses. The plausibility of such an explanation vanishes however when we remember that over-production, which seems to be an incident of all crises, must be accounted for.

Perplexed by these considerations, I have tried to probe the actual organization of industry in the hope that I might discover in it constant influences and tendencies which should result in recurrent derangements of business. The following argument is submitted diffidently. It rests upon obvious facts which no one should question. If the facts seem trite and tedious, I beg the reader to consider that one must reason from what is known and admitted rather than from disputed premises.

Part II.

Recurrent Tides in Business.—
The observed series of events which
precede and follow a crisis are
significant. After every crisis has
followed a period of readjustment.
Failures have been numerous;
many works have been shut down;
laborers have lacked employment;
profits have declined and dullness
has prevailed. During the depression competition has become keen.
Manufacturers and distributers of
goods have found it hard to sell
them and in the effort to broaden
their markets have been forced to
make goods as cheaply and sell

them as cheaply as possible. Under the stress of such pressure the cost of goods has been gradually reduced by the adoption of better machinery, better methods, better work and greater economy, and in the course of a few years, as the result of these improvements, the cost of all goods has fallen. Then has been felt a distinct improvement. A new and increasing demand has sprung up; producers have become more active, more men have been employed, trade has become easy and a stronger impulse has been felt in every branch of business. The factory, the carrier, the jobber, the merchant, the laborer have become busily engaged and a period of cheerful prosperity has succeeded to the former dullness and depression.

During this period many new works have been undertaken. The profits of business have afforded abundant capital and all sorts of enterprises have been started. Wages have advanced very rapidly; factories have been run overtime; buildings have been constructed; stocks and securties have advanced; dividends have been increased, and people have lived joyously and extravagantly. Such a condition of affairs is properly described by the word "boom." While it lasts men incline to throw moderation to the winds. Many of them speculate, and as under such circumstances speculation however silly seems profitable, all sorts of people become involved. Then something has happened for which no one was prepared. Some great

financial house or commercial
institution of established and
conspicuous standing has failed,
and the "boom" has collapsed.
Such a shock has usually resulted
in a brief but violent panic, and
after this has followed that slow
and depressing period of readjustment which I have described.

These crises have occurred at
approximately equal intervals of
time for more than two centuries
throughout what we call the civil-
ized world. Our problem is to discover why. No one who considers
can avoid the conviction that there
is something in prosperity which
tends to adversity. What is it?
Let us attempt to find out by a
careful analysis of the organization, methods and tendencies of
business.

Part III.

Organization of Industry.—At the outset, one fact of paramount importance confronts us: under the present industrial system all men are mutually dependent; everyone sells what he makes and buys what he needs. We depend upon our fellows and they upon us for the gratification of all desires. We use butter from Wisconsin, meat from Illinois, bread from Minnesota, woolen clothing from Massachusetts or England, silks from France or New Jersey, shoes from Missouri or Massachusetts, china and glass from Ohio,

Pennsylvania or Austria, silver
from Colorado, gold from Califor-
nia or South Africa or Alaska;
and all of these things are deliv-
ered to us as we have need of them
by the various persons with whom
we deal.

Where such an organization
exists it is obvious that if the
cobbler makes few or bad shoes,
or the butcher provides bad meat,
the rest must suffer. The welfare
of everybody engaged in a special-
ized industry must depend upon
the purchasing power or exchange
value of his own commodity. The
object of trade is to secure to
each maker of special goods his
just participation in the common
stock, and therefore one should get
by trade no more and no less than
he carries into it. Fair trade

alone will accomplish this result. The trader who exacts much for little, or tenders bad goods in exchange for better articles, does not do his share, and in some fashion he must be induced to mend his ways. Where, as with us, every man is free, it is obvious that we can not by law punish the lazy and idle and rapacious among us. We must therefore in some other manner persuade them to do what the general welfare requires, and we have solved this problem in a rough but on the whole satisfactory way. After a long trial of pestering and futile legal restraints and penalties, we have come at last to rely on the selfish nature of man, not only as a motive to industry but as a guide and spur to industry of the right

sort. We permit him to be free
and expect him to be selfish,
because we know that in the free-
dom and selfishness of his fellows
he will find an indomitable pressure more powerful than legisla-
tive enactments to compel him to
do his duty. To understand precisely how this pressure is exerted
we must consider the objects and
methods of production on the one
hand and of distribution on the
other.

The problem of production is to
provide at least cost the right
articles. It is not enough to produce what another needs; he must
be able to pay for it. Hats may
be ever so useful, but if they cost
$100 few can afford to wear them.

The cost of goods, all other
things being equal, depends upon

the efficiency of labor, and the efficiency of labor depends upon the skill and energy of the workman and the tools he employs. Everything is a tool which a man uses in aid of his energy. Without a tool a man can make one article in a given time; with a tool he can make five or five hundred.

The progress of modern invention has been marked by so constant an improvement in machinery that today the problem of quantitative production may be said to have been solved. Certain sorts of raw material which depend upon time for production may become scarce, but this element only of cost can not be controlled. Our present problem is rather to produce the right sort of goods.

Theoretically, the laws which

control the goods market are simple. Under the normal operation of the law of supply and demand, it should be easy to know what goods are scarce and what are abundant. If certain articles are cheap and others, costing no more in energy, are dear, industry should incline to the latter because the profit to be derived from making them is greater. There ought therefore to be a gradual but constant shifting of industry from one craft to another until all human needs shall have been satisfied at a nearly uniform profit; and in every community such a movement is observable, for there are always some men of intelligence quick to observe a want and eager to grow rich by gratifying it. If the profits of this class

become abnormally large, others
will follow and in time correct
the disparity in the supply of the
various articles needed. Where
on the other hand certain goods
are over-produced, profits decline
and production is curtailed. No
one can continue to make goods
which must be sold at a loss. And
so men are induced to make the
right goods at least cost.

The laws and methods of distribution are more involved.
Goods are cheaper as the result
of a division of labor, that is they
cost less in labor; but in order that
all workers may fairly participate
in this advantage, it is requisite
that goods shall be so distributed
as to secure to each his just part
in the common stock. Such participation is secured in a rough

way as I have said by trade.

In a former essay I attempted
to show precisely how such a distribution is normally realized. We
may readily understand the methods employed if we consider the
simplest sort of trade, or barter.
In barter we exchange goods for
goods immediately; neither party
is buyer nor seller—each is both.
Neither should derive an advantage at the cost of the other, for
the articles exchanged are pre-
sumed to be of equal value. The
benefits of the transaction must
always be mutual. Each gets
what he wants in exchange for
what he has, and this common
advantage is all that should be
intended.

Selling and buying are but
barter at one remove: goods are

exchanged for money and then money for goods, value for value; but the mutual advantage derived from trading with money is not quite so evident. To demonstrate such advantage, 1 venture to repeat what I have said elsewhere.

Barter is where shoes are exchanged for a hat. In commerce shoes are sold for money and a hat is bought with money. The identity of the two transactions so far as the effect is concerned is revealed by the following illustration: A hat is worth, say, a pair of shoes. Let me assume that the hatter and cobbler have each $5 and his own commodity. It makes no difference to either party whether the hat be bartered for the shoes or each article be sold for $5. As this principle is fundamental, I must repeat a demonstration already familiar perhaps to some of my readers.

Where a hat costs or is worth $3 and a pair of shoes $4, and the hatter sells a hat to the cobbler and the cobbler a pair of shoes to the hatter at cost, after trading each party will have property worth precisely as much as the property he started with. The whole effect of the transaction is the substitution of one sort of value for another equal value; neither party has made anything out of the other.

In trade, however, goods are never sold at cost; everybody wishes to make something by it. Each in fact does make something, but not quite what he expects. In barter, one value is compared with

another and each party estimates
the value of both commodities.
The exchange is effected because
each wants what the other has
and no profit is expected. In buying and selling, this actual profit
(and it is the only profit that can
be realized by fair trade) is hid
by the intervention of money
which seems to allow of profit of
another sort.

The hatter may say that a hat
which cost $3 is worth for sale $5,
and by selling to the cobbler at
that price seem to realize a profit
of $2; but if the cobbler is of
opinion that a pair of shoes costing $4 is worth for sale $6, and
the hatter buys at that price, the
cobbler also has made a profit of
$2. In fact neither has made any
such profit. The hatter had before

trading a hat worth $3 and say $5 in cash; after trading, he had a pair of shoes worth $4 and $4 in cash, or just as much in value as he started with, $3+5=4+4$. So did the cobbler, for he started with a pair of shoes worth $4 and $5 in cash; and after trading he has a hat worth $3 and $6 in cash —just as much as he started with. $4+5=3+6$. The profit of such trading is the acquisition of what one needs by exchange for what one has, precisely as in the case of barter.

The function of money so used is not to change, control or effect the relative values of commodities but to measure them. Where a cow is worth $50 and a sheep $5, the cow is worth ten times as much as the sheep and it matters not whether we say the cow is worth $100 or $50, always provided the sheep is valued at $10 or $5. The pecuniary profits derived from trade are deceptive because selling and buying are distinct transactions and only after having sold and bought can we know whether we have made a good or bad bargain.

A college professor has devised a plan to overcome the fluctuating money values of goods by what he calls a variable standard of value predicated upon averages. It ought not to be hard to understand that one can not make potatoes abundant or eggs scarce by alterations in the weight of a dollar.

The object then of trade is not to make money but to distribute the benefits resulting from a division of labor by a fair exchange of the goods so produced. Its prosperity depends upon the ease with which that object may be accomplished. Money makes trade in a certain sense easy, for goods may usually be sold at some price and bought at some price; yet money adds to trade the element of uncertainty above mentioned which can not be quite obviated. Where goods are sold and bought, one may unconsciously sell for less or buy for more than goods are worth. This unintended loss is mitigated in some measure by the natural propensity of every man to seek buyers who will pay most and sellers who will ask least, yet it is never quite overcome, because buying and selling

are not concurrent transactions.
The propensity to sell dear and
buy cheap has however resulted
in the establishment of instrumen-
talities which if not markets in
the old sense yet are markets in
the sense that they establish quo-
tations and notify men of the relative values of goods.

Where such facilities exist, it is
obvious that trade will be mutually profitable or otherwise as the
prices quoted are fair or not. One
can not as a rule sell too dear,
nor buy too cheap, because trades
can not be effected on such terms.
To traders who meet face to face
this fact is evident. Each will
demand what he thinks his own
goods are worth, and if after bar-
gaining the trade is consummated
it will be because both are satis-

fied. A rise or fall in the price of special goods should be the result of fluctuating market conditions which indicate but do not cause some disparity between the supply of and demand for such goods. Goods are now roughly valued for the purpose of distribution in the following manner: every trader asks as much and pays as little as possible, preferring always to deal with him who asks least and pays most. Under such circumstances the tendency of all prices should be to approximate actual values. An exact equality is never quite arrived at, but the necessary tendency of trading in an open, competitive market is toward fair dealing.

I should perhaps note for the information of the reader that

when I say trade involves no other
profit than the advantage which
results from getting what one
wants with what one makes, I am
not discussing what is called
merchandising. The profits made
by merchants are rewards for services rendered to the consumer and
producer of goods. They are paid
because merchants help men to get
what they need in exchange for
what they make. This aspect of
distribution I have discussed in
the "Meaning of Property," and
need not discuss here.

By way of recapitulation, it may
be said that industry is theoretically controlled by influences
which compel selfish men engaged
in various sorts of production to
make the right articles and offer
them for exchange on fair terms.

Part IV.

Disturbing Influences. — T h e even prosperity which should result from an organization involving production and distribution so controlled, is never altogether realized. Business in the long run is guided by irresistible laws, but its adaptations to changing conditions are sometimes slow and feeble owing to the temporary stress of disturbing influences.

Not all men are equally intelligent and equally industrious; therefore an industry dependent upon human nature is a disturbed and uneven industry. Men will not or can not always do the right thing at the right time. The practice of one trade does not fit a man for another: it is hard for a shoemaker to become a weaver; a machinist can not turn his hand to chemistry. The more intricate the machine employed, the further the division of labor is carried, the more minute and distinct the processes of manufacture, the more difficult it is for men to adjust themselves to the fluctuating demand for various articles.

Not only is labor immobile, but capital once invested in special tools for one trade has become fixed and unavailable for another. A shoe factory can not be turned into a flour mill without great loss. The theoretical development and steady progress of business are retarded and embarrassed by these hindrances. Men and capital cling to an overcrowded industry and will cling to it until forced to abandon it by the stress of necessity. The wrong goods are under such circumstances likely to be produced, that is goods for which there is so poor a market that the price offered will not pay the cost of production.

A more serious cause of disturbance is found in the enervating effects of prosperity. Where the need to work is relaxed and wages are very high, workmen become less zealous, their efficiency declines and the cost of goods increases. The master is also affected by prosperity, for where his business is brisk tools are neglected and improvements in the processes of manufacture put off. Under such circumstances both the employer and employe become obsessed by the notion that they may thrive at somebody else's expense, and each seeks to get more than he deserves. Increased wages are demanded and granted; prices are put up, and every other class of the community begins to feel the pinch of what is called the "high cost of living." The real trouble is costly production: there may not be fewer goods to go around, but some men can not pay the prices asked.

The consequences of rising prices are slow in development but inevitable. A gradual increase in the cost of goods hurts many consumers. High prices, however alluring they may seem, are not indications of a real prosperity. The purchasing power of wages and profits is the measure by which they are to be estimated; and if incomes will purchase less and less from month to month and from year to year, the prosperity which high prices seem to indicate is fictitious.

There is in every community a considerable class which is engaged neither in what we call production nor distribution. To this class belong professional men, clerks, school teachers and a multitude of detached women and others, each of whom has a relatively fixed and unalterable income. Such income has a limited purchasing power, and as prices advance this class must practice self-denial and its economy must tend to narrow the market for goods.

High prices are not only afflicting to the class whose incomes are limited but in the long run to all others however prosperous they may seem. Nothing is so easy as to advance prices during a boom, and the temptation to do so is constant and irresistible. Raw materials advance, wages advance, fuel advances, all other elements of cost advance, and the obvious thing to do is to ask more for goods. While the boom lasts profits easily made are readily spent, and no one perceives the general inconvenience which must in the course of time follow. That inconvenience results from the fact that during a boom the prices of all commodities do not advance ratably and equally,

nor do wages advance precisely in
correspondence with the cost of
living. The derangements resulting from these aberrations may be
illustrated by the effect of a good
or bad crop on the prosperity of
those who are not engaged in agri-
culture. Where food is scarce,
more of everybody's income is required to buy food and less is
available for other purposes.
Where on the contrary food is
cheap and abundant, more of
everybody's income is available for
other wants. On the other hand,
where food is cheap and other
goods are very high, the farmer
can not buy as many of such goods
as if they were cheap, and the
laborer whose wages lag behind
the general advance in prices must
buy less and less; and so in the

progress of every advance there are added to the class whose incomes are limited more and more people who must be economical, and their economy results in a gradual relaxation in the demand for expensive goods, and therefore in an arrest of the prosperity of those who produce them.

PART V.

Causes of Crises.—In none of
these considerations do we find a
wholly satisfactory explanation of
crises. Such disturbances are usually violent alterations in the
course of business affairs, attended
by a shock called a panic. A
gradual increase in the prices
asked for goods and a gradual falling off in the demand should not
result in any such catastrophe.
Trade may rise or fall under fluctuating influences, but the alterations should be rather like the
undulations of the ocean than
the occasional tidal waves which

devastate. We must therefore account for the violence and diffused consequences of crises and seek elsewhere for an adequate cause. One fact is significant.

No crisis ever occurred among a primitive or simple people. Men who barter goods for goods may be more or less prosperous, but they can not be overwhelmed by commercial crises. What then is the difference between modern commerce and the commercial dealing of our ancestors? We buy and sell on credit; they did not. Only after the use of credit became general did any crisis occur. In the use of credit we may perhaps find what we seek.

Let us first understand why credit is employed. We resort to it because the quantities of goods to be exchanged have become so enormous that we can not conveniently pay cash. If a million dollars of sales involved the payment by the purchaser of a million of dollars in cash, and all of the trade of the country had to be so conducted, we should find trade very troublesome. Checks are employed to avoid this trouble. The use of checks necessarily involves credit.

Credit is not only convenient but profitable. A merchant can make more money by buying on credit than by buying with cash. If he has one thousand dollars and buys one thousand dollars worth of goods and sells them for eleven hundred dollars, he has made in a given time say $50 after deducting the expense incurred. If on the

other hand he borrows one thousand dollars at eight per cent per
annum, he can make by credit in
the same time (say three months)
$50 less $20, or $30, without using
any money of his own.

It should be easy now to understand why influences affecting the
cost and price of goods should
result in crises. The manufacturer and the merchant are both
borrowers; they borrow to buy,
and sell on credit. Where business is dull, they borrow little;
where it is brisk, they borrow
more; where it is excited and
prices and wages increase rapidly,
they borrow a great deal. During a period of rising prices
the risk run is slight, for goods
bought can be sold and debts in-
curred can be paid from the pro-

ceeds. But if the demand for goods be suddenly arrested and prices hesitate and then break, the situation of the borrower may become perilous. He may not be able to sell his goods save at a loss, yet he must pay his debt or renew it. If he extends his debt and the decline in prices continues, his peril becomes graver. A prudent man will under such circumstances sell at a loss and take his punishment, but such selling still further depresses the goods market and by reason of such stress many imprudent men can not pay their debts. To them and to their creditors a crisis has come, violent or slight in proportion to the number so involved.

A crisis seems to be caused by a series of influences which tend to inefficient production, high cost and increasing prices upon the one hand; and upon the other to enforced economy and a falling demand for goods at the prices asked. It is occasioned by the unexpected discovery that outstanding obligations can not be paid by the sale of goods on hand.

When business is at flood tide, some great house fails and all others become alarmed. All are mutually involved. Banks owe their depositors; manufacturers owe the banks; merchants owe both. If any can not pay, credit becomes strained and if the strain be not instantly relieved a panic must follow, during which every man engaged in business trembles. No trader is safe. He may be ever so solvent, but if his debts mature and he can not collect from his debtors, or convert his goods into cash, or renew his notes, he must suspend; and so the panic spreads from insolvent to solvent, overwhelming for a moment all engaged in business.

The function of a crisis is to curb the rapacity of selfish men. If, under our free system, each industry were at liberty to extort for its own goods as much as it wished; if no inducement to economical production were afforded, and none to fair dealing, all of the advantages of specialization would be lost. No confederation between unscrupulous workmen and rapacious employers can, however, prevail over the stern and stubborn resistance of the oppressed community. There is a fair price for goods, and that price depends upon their exchange value; and none can in the long run get more for his own than they are worth to another. A crisis compels and restores fair dealing. Its effect is to compel men to work diligently. Society will buy such goods as it can afford to buy and no more, and in order to revive a demand killed by poverty goods must be brought again within the reach of the poor. A crisis accomplishes this result. It is usually violent, because men are selfish and stubborn and must be forced by violence back to mutual fair dealing.

Part VI.

Other Theories.—In order that
the simplicity of such an explanation may not repel the confidence
of the reader, I venture to compare it with what others have said
of particular crisis. Every panic
of the past has provoked discus-
sion. If what I have said be true,
it must be reconcilable with all
that has occurred ; if it be false,
we should discover its error in its
conflict with established facts.

The events which preceded
former crises, set forth in Juglar's
"History of Panics in the United

States," at page 33, were as follows:

1814. The banks, led on by thirst of gain, issued unprecedented amounts of bank notes. The depreciation of fiat money raised the price of everything. This superficial occurrence was looked upon as a real increase, and gave rise to all the consequences that a general inflation of value could produce. This mistake on the subject of artificial wealth made landed proprietors desire unusual proceeds. The villager, deceived by a demand surpassing his ordinary profits, extended his credit and filled his store with the highest-priced goods; and importations, having no other proportion to the real needs than the wishes of the retailers, soon glutted the market. Everyone wished to speculate and everyone eagerly ran up debts. Such was the abundance of paper money that the banks were alarmed lest they

could not find investments for
what they manufactured. This
state of things lasted until the end
of 1815, when it was recognized
that the paper circulation had not
enriched the community.

1819. In 1818 speculation was
so wild that no one failed on account of a smaller sum than
$100,000. A drawing-room that
had cost $40,000 and a bankrupt's
wine cellar estimated to have cost
$7,000 were cited as instances of
prodigality. On the thirteenth of
December, 1819, a committee of
the House of Representatives reported that the panic extended
from the greatest to the smallest
capitalists. Those who unfortu-
nately owed money lost all the
fruit of long work, and skilled
laborers were obliged to exchange
the shelter of their old homes for
the inhospitable western forests.
Forced sales of provisions, merchandise and implements were
made greatly below their purchase
price. Many families were obliged

to limit their most necessary
wants. Money and credit were so
scarce that it became impossible
to obtain loans upon lands with
the securest titles. Work ceased
with its pay, and the most skillful
workman was brought to misery.
Trade was restricted to the nar-
rowest wants of life. Machinery
and factories were idle. The debtors' prison overflowed. (Pages 50
and 51.)

1829. In 1824 in Pennsylvania
there was a new rage for banks,
and in 1825 there was a repetition
of the marvelous days of 1815. A
bill was passed re-establishing the
charters of all banks which had
failed in 1814. Ready money was
never so abundant. There was a
panic in England in 1825, the most
severe that England had ever ex-
perienced. In 1829 the Bank of
New York claimed to have so much
money that it did not know what
to do with it. The following years
the banks extended their opera-
tions, and a rise in prices accom-

panied the ease of getting credit;
but in November of 1831, very
urgent demands for money were
heard. American writers boasted
greatly about the assistance the
Bank of the United States yielded
business and the nation. (Pages
57 and 58.)

1837. In 1833 President Jackson ordered the withdrawal of
government deposits from the
Bank of the United States. Deposits were withdrawn and placed
in different State banks and the
Bank of the United States was
obliged to limit its discounts and
loans, thus causing trouble. President Jackson and his successor,
Van Buren, considered the excessive issue of paper money the
principal cause of the panic, as
well as the over-doing of every
branch of trade, the boundless
speculation, the increase of foreign debts, imprudent land specu-
lations, alarming increase of a
luxury fatal to the springs of industry and to the morality of the

people. In 1836 imports exceeded exports by fifty millions, which had to be paid for in gold or silver. The outflow of metal created a great void. The advance in the discount rates in the Bank of England came like a thunder clap and the distended bladder burst; banks suspended payment; bank notes lost from ten to twenty per cent; cotton fell to nothing. At the beginning of April, 1837, the New York banks suspended. The United States Bank suspended in the same year. The panic from 1837 to 1839 produced, according to some pretty accurate reports of 1841, 33,000 failures involving a loss of $440,000,000. (Page 80.)

1848. Banks increased from 691 in 1843 to 751 in 1848, and their capital grew from $196,-000,000 to $207,000,000. Paper circulation rose from $58,000,000 to $128,000,000. The metallic reserve fell from $49,000,000 in 1844 to $35,000,000 in 1848. The panic was slight and did not cause much trouble. The liquidation of the panic of 1837 was barely over and was still too recent to permit of excessive business extension. Embarrassments were slight and brief. (Page 81.)

1857. The stoppage of 1848 was brief. Discounts rose steadily from $332,000,000 to $684,000,-000. The circulation rose from $114,000,000 to $214,000,000; the capital of the banks, from $196,-000,000 to $370,000,000. In 1857 the cash on hand was $1 in hard money for each, $8 in paper. Banks had attracted deposits by high rates of interest, and loaned money to wild speculators. The collapse of the Ohio Life Co., which has the best New York connections, was the first muttering of the storm, and was soon followed by the suspension of the Mechanics Banking Association, one of the oldest banks in the country. (Page 84.) At the height of the crisis failures were so numerous that a general suspension of payments and in consequence a stoppage of all business was dreaded. The banks suspended payment upon a common understanding. The critical moment was passed and tranquillity reappeared. (Page 88.)

1873. During the last two months of 1872 the American market had been very much embarrassed. The lowest rate of discount was seven per cent, and in December it was quoted at a quarter of one per cent a day. The year 1873 was anxiously awaited in hope of better times. On the first days of April the market was in full panic. It grew steadier in the first week of May and in the months following. It relapsed in September, and broke forth on September 18th through the failure of J. Cook, after a miserable year during which money was constantly sought for and held at very high prices in all branches of business. (Page 94.) Fifty-one hundred concerns failed, with liabilities of $300,000,000.

1884. The panic which burst upon the United States in 1884 was the last thunder clap of the commercial tempest which had reigned since the month of January, 1882. Public opinion already recalled the decennial period which separated the existing panic from that of 1873. The acute period was of short duration. The crash occurred on May 14th and the decline in values had touched bottom by the end of June. From the ninth of June people began to steady up and they felt the ground firmer under their feet. The situation gave evidence of strength; notwithstanding an enormous fall in prices, there were only a few failures. The losses were entirely borne by financiers and speculators. (Page 102.)

1893. The following facts are taken from the History of the Crises under the National Bank System, published by Congress:

The Reading Railroad failed February 26, 1893, and its failure gave rise to doubts of other companies, particularly of the industrials. The tendency of call rates was high. The National Cordage Company failed in May. The New York market suffered a severe shock panic. Commercial paper was quoted from six to nine per cent. It was argued that business was being deprived of needed capital, but the returns of the banks showed no contraction whatever, but rather the contrary. (Pages 163-165.) A withdrawal of money from the New York banks was due to the failure of large numbers of banks, both State and National. Nineteen National banks were placed in the hands of receivers. Some banks went to the wall in consequence of many commercial failures, 3,401 in number, with liabilities of $169,000,000. Banks, with few exceptions, suspended payment and resorted to clearing house certificates. (Page 170.)

Commodity prices continued to fall. August witnessed a decline in general business activities. Contraction in loans was perhaps the most striking feature of the crisis. (Page 208.) As always when general trade depression sets in, the banks soon found themselves with abundant funds.

Crisis of 1907. This crisis was preceded by no liquidation or monetary conditions unfavorable to sound banking. On the contrary, these influences tended to strengthen the banks. (Page 216.) In 1906 there were indications that the pace was too rapid and that economic forces were becoming unstable. The San Francisco earthquake destroyed an immense amount of capital (page 237), but even if it had not occurred it is certain that the demand for capital was outstripping current savings. When corporations of the highest standing were obliged to resort to short-time notes, it was evident that other corporations were expanding upon an insufficient foundation. (Page 238.) Another indication of declining trade was the increasing ratio of cost reported in many industries. The incompetent could hold places because there were none to fill their positions. (Page 239.) The declaration of a dividend by the Southern Pacific Railroad Company gave encouragement to the unbridled optimism. (Page 239.) There was a rich man's panic in March, 1907. The price of copper fell from 26 cents a pound to 13 cents in October. (Page 242.) On account of the increased cost of living and extravagant expenditure, there was a decline in savings and borrowers of all kinds had difficulty in securing capital. (Page 243.) October 21st the Knickerbocker Trust Company, the third largest in New York, failed. (Page 251.) The course of events proved that general economic conditions were not unsound. (Page 274.) Mercantile failures were not very large. Banks suspended payment almost universally. Commodity prices fell.

Mr. Thom, the translator and editor of Mr. Juglar's book, condenses Mr. Juglar's theories in the following words: "A crisis or panic may be defined as a stoppage of the rise of prices, that is to say the period when new buyers can not be found. It is always accompanied by a reactionary movement in prices. A panic may be broadly stated as due to overtrading which causes general business to need more than the available capital, thus producing lack of credit." (Page 13.)

The symptoms of approaching panic generally patent to everyone are: Wonderful prosperity, indicated by various and numerous

enterprises and schemes of all
sorts; a rise in the prices of all
commodities, lands, houses, etc.;
an active request for workmen; a
rise in salaries; a lowering of
rates of interest; gullibility of the
public; a general taste for speculating in order to grow rich at
once; a growing luxury leading
to excessive expenditure; a very
large amount of discounts and a
very small reserve specie. (Page
9.)

The following extracts are taken
from the appendix to Mr. Burton's
work on Crises and Depression
(page 311) :

Walter Bagehot: At particular
times, a great many stupid people
have a great deal of stupid money.
At intervals, from causes which
are not to the present purpose, the
money of these people, the blind
capital, is particularly large and
craving. It seeks for someone to
devour it. It finds someone, there

is speculation, and it is devoured, and there is a panic.

McPherson: At times the concerns of merchants and manufacturers were very much more widely extended and were much greater than at any former period—an actual effect of increasing prosperity and sometimes a cause of ensuing calamity.

Horace White: Speculation, the act of buying with a view to selling at a higher price, and over-trade or the act of buying and selling too much on a given capital. Most commonly the two elements are accompanied by two others, to-wit: the destruction or loss of previously accumulated capital and the rapid conversion of circulating into fixed capital. Speculation and the destruction of capital usually go together and prepare for a crisis.

Price: A nation grows rich by increase of capital, by applying their wealth, improving their ma-

chinery and increasing the facilities for production. Nations grow
poor by consuming more than
they have made, by diminishing
those things which keep alive industry and cause goods to be
made. The reasons why people do
not buy is the lack of some commodity which can be exchanged
for money and then used for purchasing. What is the foundation
of ill? The cause is over-consum-
ing, destroying more wealth than
is produced. The necessary consequence is poverty.

Clark: Before every commercial crisis there is a period during
which there takes place very much
production that does not cater to
normal and permanent wants and
therefore can not continue. Much
production needs to be checked by
the harsh operation of a crisis.

Leroy Beaulieu says that crises
proceed from "great specialization of production, the division of
labor—a division which is not
alone personal but territorial—

the habitual dependence of production upon consumption, the active role of speculation and of a credit which stretches the economic spring sometimes to extremes, very profound modifications in the principal branches of production —particularly following a great technical progress effected upon one point or another—the sudden and permanent increase in considerable proportions of certain categories of products of a nature such that the habitual proportions between offer and demand are very much modified."

Rogers: The cause of a crisis exists in the function of exchange, in the expectation of unreasonable profits.

Griffen: The explanation is the condition of prices for years past. Usually a great depression succeeds a great period of inflation. A fall of prices is a usual feature in every depressed period, and accentuates and very largely creates depression.

Marshall: The more complete and philosophical solution of the problem is found in the constitution of human nature itself, which bears with impatience the dullness of a monotonous level and rapidly passes from one extreme to the other. Enthusiasm and despondency are equally epidemic. When prices are rising and profits (even when only on paper) roll up rapidly, everybody is eager to buy; but when this eagerness has evaporated and suspicion succeeds to confidence, the current turns the other way: everybody desires to sell, and prices fall.

James Wilson: We are more than ever convinced that the fluctuating character of the cost of the first and imperative necessities of life is the chief cause of the whole derangement of financial and commercial interests in a great country. It is not to high prices nor to low prices that we attribute the evils complained of, but to a constant and incessant changeableness, to periods of fluctuation and to a series of years of cheapness followed by years of high prices.

Lawson: The cause is to be attributed to a sudden check given to an extensive and long-continued trading upon credit.

Easton: In times of prosperity credit is abused, and by this means the trader incurs liabilities which he is unable to meet. This leads to a crisis.

Edward Everett: If I mistake not, the distress of the year 1857 was produced by an enemy more formidable than hostile arms, by pestilence more deadly than fever or plague, by a visitation more destructive than the frosts of spring or the blights of summer. I believe it was caused by a mountain load of debt.

Wallace: Depressions of trade may be succinctly defined as a widespread diminution of a demand for our chief manufactures both at home and abroad.

Howe: We may finish this summing up by adding that the principal cause, stated in the fewest possible words, consists in the blind misdirection of energy, enterprise, labor and capital.

If we compare these various dicta, we shall find it difficult to reconcile them, unless we remember that they present points of view merely. I think that all of them may be reconciled. None invalidate the conclusion at which I had arrived. Before every panic, prices have advanced and then a strain has been felt in the money market. No one has thought it worth while to explain the correlation between these two facts. Mr. Lawson contents himself with saying "Crises are to be attributed to a sudden-check given to extensive trading on credit." Mr. Wal-

lace attributes a crisis to "a widespread diminution of demand for
our chief manufactures." Mr.
Wilson is convinced that the fluctuating cost of the necessaries of
life is the chief cause of the derangement of financial and commercial affairs. Mr. Leroy Beaulieu thinks crises proceed from the
"division of labor, the dependence
of production upon consumption,
and the sudden and permanent
increase in certain categories of
products which disturbs the habitual proportion between supply
and demand." Many mention
over-production, several speculation, as the immediate cause of
crisis. None of these opinions
should disturb the suggestion under consideration, namely, that
commercial crises are caused by

the growing disparity between the debts payable by traders and the market value of their goods.

PART VII.

*Test of Theory by Bank State-
ments.*—We should not however
rely upon mere opinion in order
to test the validity of any economic theory. If falling prices
tend to insolvency under certain
circumstances, the fact should be
reflected in the bank statements.
These statements show what the
banks owe their depositors and
what borrowers owe the banks.
The two items should always approximate equality, because deposits furnish the loanable funds
of the banks. If before a crisis
deposits decline and discounts in-

crease, until the disparity between them has reached considerable proportions, we have a right to conclude that there is some connection between the crisis and the disparity. Profits made by traders should swell the resources of the banks. Where such resources decline during a period of active trade, we must conclude that trade is for some reason unprofitable, and such conclusion is confirmed if at the same time discounts increase. The merchant who can not pay his debts and expenses with the proceeds of his goods must borrow more and deposit less.

An example of a deranged situation is afforded by the statement of the New York banks for the month of November, 1906. The loans then amounted to $1,044,000,000; deposits to $982,000,000; and reserves were $6,000,000 less than the law required. Call money reached thirty-six per cent in the first, twenty-eight per cent in the second, 29 per cent in the third and eighteen per cent in the fourth week of November. Such stress did not correct the situation. In the month of November, 1907, the loans were $1,180,000,000; deposits $1,074,000,000 and reserves $46,000,000 less than the law required. In the meantime a crisis occurred which culminated in the October panic of that year.

What these statements show with respect to the situation just before the crisis of 1907, the statements of all banks show with respect to the period which has

preceded every crisis that has
occurred. Always deposits have
been less than discounts, and
always reserves have been less than
they should have been, and always
high rates of interest have failed
to correct the balance.

I do not mean to attribute all
periods of stress in the money
market to the condition of trade
alone. Very acute financial panics
may be occasioned by speculation.
The panic of 1869 resulted from
speculation in gold, and the brief
panic of 1903 from speculation in
stocks of newly organized trusts
called "undigested" securities.
Such speculation is usually a con-
comitant of all crisis, but ought
not to be so widespread as to cause
one. Where prices rise and men
make money easily, they incline

to venture something and so invest
their surplus earnings in hazard-
ous enterprises; but such speculation, which is the effect of prosperity, should not of itself arrest
prosperity unless it be so extensive as to induce the waste of
more than merchants can afford
to lose. No such waste is ever
observable. Few merchants actually become insolvent. After the
panic is over, business is resumed
but always on a falling price
market. Goods do not become
cheap and stay so merely because
formerly earned profits have been
wasted or badly invested by a
small class of speculators, however sharply securities may be
affected by such folly.

The argument afforded by bank
statements is fortified by reflec-

tion. The banks are after all but organized media of exchange. Men borrow from them in order to buy, and deposit in them after sale. Where business is good and trade profitable, it is obvious that deposits must increase. It is equally obvious that where business is arrested and profits can not be realized, deposits must diminish and discounts increase. Merchants who can not sell goods yet must nevertheless pay their expenses, draw out their balances or borrow more. Falling prices tend to these results.

The theory which I venture to suggest seems therefore to be plausible. Nothing said by close observers of many such disturbances tends to weaken it, and it is confirmed not only by the state-

ments of the banks just before
every crisis, but by what seems to
be the natural and inevitable
tendency of the high cost of goods
on the one hand and the arrested
demand for such goods on the
other. Moreover, after every crisis
the market prices of all goods have
steadily declined and failures have
become more and more numerous;
and these facts indicate a readjustment following the contrary
tendency.

The theory allows for the free
play of all the factors of disaster
mentioned by the writers quoted:
for inflation, speculation, credit
distension, tight money, waste,
unreasonable profits. high cost of
living, abuse of credit, misdirected
energy, fall in prices and over-
production. Every one of these

considerations is reconcilable with the assumption that crises are caused by inefficient production, high cost, an arrested demand for goods at the prices asked and the inability of those engaged in business to pay their debts under such circumstances with the proceeds of goods on hand. Over-production, which seems irreconcilable with the theory, in fact confirms it in a striking manner; for what men call "over-production" means in fact production at a cost which men can not afford to pay. As soon as the price is reduced, there is always a ready demand for the goods "over-produced."

Part VIII.

The Coming Crisis.—No one can regard the present industrial and financial situation without a certain apprehension. Money is tight, the currency of the country is enormously inflated, deposits are declining, discounts are increasing, wages and profits are excessively high, production is inefficient, goods cost more than ever before, prices are exorbitant, many men are speculating, a tremendous amount of capital is being wasted by municipalities and other public corporations, taxes are oppressive, the waste of the war still continues, foreign trade is withdrawing from the country billions more goods than are being imported, the debts of foreign nations to us can not be immediately paid, Europe is wretchedly poor, and in the face of these disturbing influences, the wildest extravagance and the most pinching economy are everywhere evident.

The reader who examines the histories of other crises will discover nothing even approximating the disorder which now confronts us. We have put out more paper money than ever before; prices of commodities are higher than ever before; more wealth has been and is being wasted than ever before; and more men feel the pinch of high prices than ever before. If we compare the influences which control production and distribution, we shall discover that never before was there such a disparity between the supply of and demand for goods. No manufacturer need now compete with another—competition in trade has ceased: the problem of business is not to sell but to buy. The profits derived from such a market, although enormous, seem to be unavailable for trade. Much is being spent in speculation. More and more money is being borrowed. The crisis of 1873, following our Civil War and the War of 1870 between France and Germany, was devastating and prolonged, yet the influences which conduced to it were less powerful than those which are now in operation. Such considerations are ominous.

Before making up our minds, let us carefully weigh and consider the various factors of disaster with which we have to reckon. If it be true that crises are due to the disparity between the debts payable by traders and the market values of their goods, we can perceive no cause for immediate alarm. All goods can now be sold instantly and at a profit, and all debts can be promptly paid. Collections are easy and failures are few. Why then should we view the future with apprehension? First, because every period of similar prosperity came to an abrupt and shocking end; second, because we feel in a vague way that business is now abnormal in the sense that it was never before so easy to get rich nor so hard to escape poverty.

If we add to these general considerations others which can not be ignored, apprehension becomes confirmed. The production of all goods has been stimulated by the highest prices on record, yet the supply is still deficient. Whence proceeds a demand for very expensive goods which can not be satisfied? From our own spenders, from the various taxing authorities, from the peoples of Europe; and all these demands are abnormal. The extravagant are spending profits made during the war, or gains derived from current high prices; the cities, towns, States and United States are appropriating by taxation more and more goods from year to year; the distress of the people of Europe compels them to buy beyond their means. The demand so originating can not last. It is not an economic or normal demand.

Ordinarily if I buy a barrel of flour I give for it goods of another kind but of equal value. What I appropriate from the general stock I give an equivalent value for. But today there is no such reciprocal trade. Profiteers get more than they give; the government gets all for nothing; Europeans can not pay. Even the fabulous fortunes made during the war will some time be expended or invested. Taxes must decline, else industry will decay; the buying of Europeans has reached a limit; their credit is exhausted.

When such demands shall have been checked, what should be the consequences? The first effect should be a relaxation in the tension of business, the second a softening in prices, the third a decline in profits, and the fourth an increasing demand for money to pay debts. If to these tendencies we add the importation of goods from abroad to pay for those already bought or other goods needed, and an inevitable effort of the reserve system to deflate currency by forcing sales of merchandise, is it not obvious that the boom must collapse?

If any doubt still remains, it should be dispelled by the following indisputable facts: During 1919 we exported four billions more than we imported; the cost and prices of commodities were higher than ever before; the profits made in trade were greater than ever before, yet the statements of the New York banks for December 6, 1919, showed discounts of $5,155,327,000 and demand deposits of $4,132,911,000; or a ratio of one hundred and twenty-five per cent, notwithstanding the tremendous profits derived from trade. In December, 1919, the notes of the federal reserve banks amounted to $2,700,000,000 and still money was tight.

So remarkable a situation was never before encountered. Yet I do not mean to cause an inconsiderate anxiety. It is always foolish to take a partial view of the very numerous considerations which constitute an economic situation. There are other facts which must be taken into account. In all probability the actual wealth of the United States has not been greatly impaired by the war. We sold goods to Europe at an enormous profit, and redeemed all of our foreign debts and now have a balance due us of many billions. Reserve notes are still convertible into gold, the profiteers of all classes, employers and laborers, have perhaps still billions of profits to waste. An immediate resumption of imports on a great scale is altogether unlikely because foreign nations are poor and need for themselves all that they can make.

Nevertheless a reaction is inevitable some time. Deflation must begin, imports must be resumed, extravagance must cease. When these factors of reaction shall begin to operate, prices must fall, trade must become less and less profitable and the disparity between the debts of the merchants and the current values of their goods must tend to widen. It is altogether probable that under such circumstances a crisis can not be avoided. Not only must the redemption of reserve notes be affected by sales of merchandise, but as the currency contracts values measured in currency must fall. Europe must pay the interest upon its debts in goods and in order to hereafter get what it needs must send other goods in exchange. Imports under such circumstances must exceed exports. Moreover Europe needs gold to rehabilitate its currencies, and as we have the only stock in the world from which gold may be drawn, it must resort to us, and the export of gold must result in still further currency contraction.

Part IX.

Caution Necessary.—Such considerations justify a policy of caution. If today we can perceive no sympton of storm, nevertheless the sky may become suddenly overcast. The barometer is disturbed. Heretofore business has never been prepared for even an imminent crisis. Business has always been most active and deemed most profitable when in greatest peril. Premonitions have never been lacking, but men have always refused to heed them. No crisis could have arisen if everybody had anticipated it. The warning conveyed by the abnormal situation which I have described will in all likelihood be disregarded. We dislike to anticipate trouble when we are making money.

The banks, which should be most cautions, are tempted to be otherwise, for when money is tight rates of interest are unusually high and it requires cool, calculated courage to withstand the temptations of the moment. No bank has heretofore been in position to make a profit by prudence. To hoard money by restricting lending is not only to offend borrowers and lose an income but to accumulate reserves which can not be retained. A run upon a bad bank induces withdrawals from one that is sound; and where loss is the inevitable consequence of caution, prudence is flung to the winds. In 1873, 1893 and 1907, all banks suspended. They lost nothing by doing so; on the contrary, the panic resulting from universal bank suspension has been most profitable to the banks. During a crisis they pay little to their depositors and exact market rates from their borrowers. Recently the banks have been tempted to great imprudence by the profits of rediscounts.

Whether the reserve system will be well managed remains to be seen. If it shall fail to do its duty, it is altogether probable that the coming crisis will be unusually severe. Banks have come to think they have a right to fall back on the reserve banks. The system is called a reserve system. It was established to avoid crises and promised that none should occur. The private banks are no longer required to carry an adequate reserve, because such reserves are to be provided by the reserve system. Under such circumstances temptations to reckless banking may be found irresistible. Whether the resources of the reserve banks will be enough to avert trouble remains to be ascertained. Their most mobile resource is notes, yet to issue notes is to inflate credit and currency when credit is most strained and therefore most unsafe. We may assume that those in authority will do whatever is requisite, but where a desire for gain has not induced prudence it is altogether unlikely that mere disinterested altruism will compel it.

Prudent men of business should not rely upon any system, however cunningly devised, to overcome the effects and consequences of bad business. Those who have become insolvent by reason of stupidity or inexperience or rashness can not be rescued by further trust. A bad debt is not paid by a fresh note, nor can an unsalable stock of goods be made profitable by delay when the market is falling.

PART X.

Indications of Trouble—How to Judge of a Situation.—We are now brought face to face with the problem which most concerns us. Assuming that a crisis will occur, how distinct and what will be the premonitions of its approach and what should a prudent merchant do who apprehends its coming?

In the first place we must bear in mind the fact that the present situation is altogether abnormal. The influences which ordinarily control business are now complicated by numerous factors which had their origin in the most wasteful war of history. That sort of inefficiency in production which results from moderate prosperity is insignificant in comparison with the lassitude which has resulted from the sudden and great enrichment of all persons engaged in business. War wages and war profits have demoralized the people and never before has the per capita output of the average factory or mine been so small.

Prices are higher than ever before, not only because it costs more to produce goods than ever before but because there are more spenders in the market than ever before. The exactions of the tax-gatherer are levied in goods, and taxes were never so heavy. Foreign nations lack necessities and their credit has been strained to the uttermost in order that they may live pending the restoration of their industries.

Three hundred billions of the capital of the world have been consumed by the war, and capital is excessively scarce at the very time when it is most needed. Rates of interest are abnormally high.

The currencies of all nations have been inflated and to other grave complications has been added the excessive inconvenience resulting from the use of fluctuating media of exchange.

On the other hand, these things must be considered. The normal increase in the population of the world has been retarded by the war; its natural resources have not been destroyed; its fields are still fertile, its mines have not been exhausted. After the commotion caused by radical alterations in systems and theories of government shall have subsided and the trade of the world shall have been resumed, men will again become industrious, and hungry men are ever most diligent.

The stress of demand on production, the tendency of high prices and great profits to stimulate industry, are now operating to induce enlargements of plants. The inefficiency of labor is compelling the introduction of labor-saving machinery.

The credit of Europeans is exhausted. In a little while they must ship goods to us in order to pay interest on their debts, and other goods in order to get what they need. Our imports will increase and exports diminish.

All of these influences co-operating will tend to an increasing supply of the necessaries of life and to a steady decline in the prices of such commodities. If we add to them the necessary effect of a gradual deflation in the currencies of the world, it is difficult to avoid the conclusion that a fall in the market prices of many goods will soon begin and steadily continue.

If a crisis be due to a series of influences which tend to inefficient production, high cost and advancing prices on the one hand, and to enforced economy, a falling demand and falling prices for goods on the other; and a panic to the unexpected discovery that on a falling market the outstanding debts of traders can not be paid in due course with available resources, then in order to judge of a situation we should consider first the goods market and then the credit market.

The goods market is now characterized by the following significant deviations from the normal:

1. Wages and profits are extravagantly high.

2. Production is inefficient.

3. The cost of goods is very great.

4. Prices are very high.

5. The demand for goods can not be satisfied.

6. Many people are afflicted by the high cost of living.

The money market is no less abnormal.

1. An immense amount of capital has been wasted in war.

2. Billions of goods have been sold to foreigners on credit.

3. Billions of capital are being wasted by the United States, the States and municipalities.

4. Taxation is preventing the accumulation of capital.

5. Capital is being wasted by speculation.

6. The currency of all countries is greatly inflated.

7. The money market is deranged; money is tight and rates of interest are high.

Each of these facts suggest a derangement in current affairs which must somehow be corrected; altogether they compel the conviction that a reaction can not be avoided. The influences which in time must bring about a reaction are obvious.

1. Decreasing exports and increasing imports.

2. Gradual deflation of the currency.

3. Export of gold.

4. Diminishing extravagance at home.

5. A fall in the prices of goods.

6. A relaxation in trade.

7. An increasing stress in the money market.

On the other hand we should not overlook very important considerations which make for delay and compel the conviction that the reaction will not occur in the near future.

1. America was enriched by the war.

2. Europe is prostrate and time will be required for its rehabilitation.

3. Goods are still scarce here and abroad.

4. Exports from Europe to us on a great scale can not be immediately resumed.

5. Many people are preparing for a reaction and their precau-

tions will tend to defer or mitigate it.

6. Several years have usually
elapsed after every former war
before a crisis has occurred.

Part XI.

Barometers.—The premonitions of coming trouble are numerous and distinct, however hard it may be to interpret them. Perhaps the following principles will afford a clue which will enable the average man to anticipate a catastrophe:

1. Where the money, or money and currency of a country remain stationary, high or low prices indicate scarcity or abundance of goods.

2. Where under such circumstances prices advance, rates of interest should advance, and where prices fall rates of interest should fall because: more or less money or credit is required to buy goods,

and where the supply of money
and credit is limited, rates depend upon the demand. Rates are
therefore as a rule high when
goods are scarce and expensive,
and low when goods are abundant
and cheap.

3. Where after an advance,
prices halt but rates of interest
continue to advance, something is
wrong. To ascertain what is
wrong we must bear in mind the
object of borrowing and the risk
of lending under various circumstances. The object of borrowing
is to make money by trade; the
risk in lending depends upon the
ability of the borrower to accomplish such object. Where prices
are advancing, it is easy to realize
a profit; where they are arrested,
it is more difficult; where they
fall, profits can not be realized.

4. A fall in prices accompanied
by a rise in interest rates indicates
that trade has become unprofitable and that under such circumstances the risk in lending is more

influential than the diminishing demand for money to buy goods.

5. A crisis is imminent when trade has ceased to be profitable; and an indication of its coming may be found in an arrest in the upward movement of prices and an advance in interest rates.

A fairly trustworthy barometer of trade conditions may therefore be found in commodity prices and rates of interest on commercial paper. Where a rise in prices is arrested and rates continue to advance, trouble may be expected. Where prices fall and rates advance still further, trouble is imminent.

Today, January 1920, the demand for goods is still excessive. Exports still exceed imports. Prices have not begun to fall. Rates of interest have not yet become excessively high and foreign exchange is still greatly depreciated. Such a situation should not cause alarm. If trouble be inevitable, it is still some way off.

If to these considerations we add the accumulated resources of merchants who made a great deal of money during the war, it is likely that a crisis will be later rather than sooner than we expect. The war of 1861-65 was profitable to traders, and in all probability what they accumulated during the war enabled them to withstand the first impact of the fall in prices which followed 1865. A crisis did not occur until 1873. Very many men have made money during the war of 1914-18. The danger which threatens them is not so great as that which followed the Civil War, for immediately after that war imports were resumed and the fall in prices which began in 1865 was in some measure at least due to imports. Our exports today continue large, and imports have not yet been resumed upon a scale which can threaten the market prices of domestic goods. After a fall shall have actually begun, time enough will be afforded for the adoption of proper precautions. The present general uncertainty has induced prudence in every department of business; if that policy be persisted in, the crisis may be deferred for a considerable period and perhaps so mitigated as to accomplish its necessary work without the shocking disturbances which usually

characterize such reactions. What
men should look for is a relaxed
demand for goods and rising rates
of interest. Warned by these indications of derangement they need
not suffer disaster.

There are other indications of
the trend and twist of business
affairs which should be helpful.
For example, the foreign exchange
market shows the fluctuations of
international commerce. Where
exchange is appreciating, it is
because the exports of Europe
are less than its imports. Where
such exchange is appreciating, it
is because the exports of Europe
to this country are increasing and
its imports are falling off, and such
a tendency can result in but one
thing: a lessening demand for
our goods abroad and a greater

supply of goods in this country. Sometimes a useful sign may be found in the bond market. During a period of prosperity every prudent merchant invests part of his profits in bonds. When business ceases to be profitable, these bonds are thrown upon the market. A crisis is so indicated months before a panic occurs. Other indications called barometers are much spoken of. Every merchant will know how to judge of them. A clever merchant declared that when he could get immediate deliveries he would go out of business. His quip suggests what has never yet occurred, namely that the market for goods distinctly softens just before a crisis. The contrary seems always to have been true: that trade is at

flood-tide just before a crash—
why, it is hard to say; perhaps
because until some notoriously
strong house collapses collections
continue good and traders are con-
fident.

The reader who attempts to
weigh in the balance so many im-
ponderable considerations will find
it hard to know which way lies
the truth. I will not venture a
conjecture. To me a crisis is some
time inevitable, but when it will
occur I can not predict. The factors of trouble are numerous and
powerful, but on the other hand
those corrective influences which
must ultimately bring down the
cost and price of goods may be
deferred for a considerable time.

To enjoin prudence under such
circumstances may be to induce a

losing caution. Men who do the business of the world can not cease to buy merely because they may in future encounter trouble. One thing may be said confidently: what all men are prepared for is not likely to happen when they expect it. To be prudent, to become strong as possible, to save, accumulate, reduce liabilities and stocks, and prepare for falling prices some time, is all that a merchant can accomplish, and enough for his safety. Unhappily, many foolish people are engaged in business who will take none of these precautions. These none can help. What they can not pay, merchants must lose. To allow for such a loss should be possible.

This then is the sum and substance of what I have written. If crises are due to inefficient production, high cost and increasing prices upon the one hand, and to enforced economy and a falling demand for goods upon the other, no crisis should occur until goods shall have been produced which can not be disposed of at the prices asked. Goods are still very scarce. The waste of the war was enormous. Billions of capital have been destroyed. Its accumulation has been retarded by the imposition of taxes which are injurious in the highest degree to the general welfare. Public and private extravagance is still unchecked, notwithstanding the high cost of living. The profits of business are still exorbitantly high and no relaxation in the demand for goods can be perceived. Many have been destroyed; the void to be filled is immense.

On the other hand, a stimulated industry is enormously productive. Every wheel in the country is turning. Europe can not continue to get without giving. In time production will overtake the demand and then business will hesitate, the rise in prices will be arrested and we shall again confront an inevitable reaction.

I have attempted to prove that there is in prosperity a tendency which results in a crisis, to show what that tendency is, how it works a general injury, why it must be corrected and how it is corrected. If what I have said be true, we should expect the future not with fear but with hope. No good man can regard the present situation with complacency. However prosperous he may be, he cannot ignore the misfortunes of that very large class which is afflicted by the high cost of living. A narrow and restricted prosperity is not the ideal of any Christian community, and none among us should deplore the operation of economic laws which tend to correct such injustice by restoring to all men a fair and no more than a fair recompense for their services; even though these laws may diminish the gains which result from high prices. Those who are wise can prepare for a reaction which is some time inevitable, and their caution should soften the blow when it comes and alleviate its chastisement.

Part XII.

How to Avert Panics.—Many
men believe we shall have no more
crises. I can not agree with them.
Panics may be averted, but the
wholesome correction of crises can
not be dispensed with. Industry
must from time to time be purged
of the incompetent. If somehow
wasteful, foolish, rapacious men
were not got rid of, production
and distribution would fall far
short of that efficiency and mutual
advantage which the general welfare demands. Panics can be
averted. None however but those
possessed of great judgment and

courage and power can control the commercial affairs of a great nation. The Bank of England arrested the panic of 1890 and mitigated the greater crisis of 1866. In France there are no panics, but crises have been frequent. Its commercial credits are never so distended as with us, and the power of the Bank of France is almost absolute. In order to avert a panic in America, the National Reserve Board must know when there is danger and use proper precautions. Such precautions are obvious.

The general use of credit in trade and the misuse of this credit are the undoubted causes of crises. One who buys with his own cash and sells for cash can not become insolvent; he may make nothing, but he can not lose everything. If however he buys on credit what he must sell at a loss, and many others do the same thing, and as a consequence of forced selling goods rapidly decline in value, all of them are overwhelmed by a common calamity.

The Reserve Board will in all probability at the right time put pressure upon imprudent buying and borrowing by reducing discounts. Heretofore it has encouraged reckless trading by discounting commercial paper at less than the market rates, and continued to inflate the currency notwithstanding the effect of inflation upon the prices of commodities. Notes which should afford a refuge in time of disaster only, have been freely used to finance a trade

already provided with abundant
resources. If a crisis shall arise,
the system may find it hard to
afford funds enough for reassur-
ance. It has lent not only the resources required to be deposited
with it by the member banks, but
much besides.

It has recently changed its
policy and advanced the rates upon
commercial paper to a parity with
market rates. What it will hereafter do no man can conjecture.
There is a danger in putting sudden pressure upon a commercial
situation, for it may provoke the
very calamity which it was designed to avert. Banks are reluc-
tant to submit to coercion. A
boom is very profitable to them.
To restrain them, to dominate
them, to deny them, requires the

122

greatest firmness backed by reasons so cogent that none but very foolish men will dare to complain.

The responsibilities of the Reserve Banks have become very heavy. Enormous credits have been granted to Europe and various groups of financiers are now urging further advances. To trust further where old debts can not be collected would seem to be fatuous to a merchant, but it seems the highest wisdom to many lenders of money. Everybody is complaining of the high cost of living and each day the papers and professors counsel economy, yet our prices are still advancing. When to the inevitable consequences of a diminished demand for domestic goods is added the stress of increasing imports from

Europe, prices will yield. When gold begins to go out, the currency must be contracted. When rediscounts are refused, merchants must sell in order to pay. The combined influence of these factors of reaction must some day be confronted. As they can not be resisted, wisdom requires that their effects shall be palliated by resort to every expedient suggested by the past. One of these expedients has recently been adopted. The task to be performed is delicate in the extreme. The solvent must be segregated from the insolvent. No one deserving help should be denied it, but those who can not be rescued must be put out of business.

Heretofore both of these tasks have been found practicable elsewhere by the use of accumulated reserves. When Overend, Gurney & Co. failed, the Bank of England paid out instantly to solvent traders all of its reserves and by free lending immediately restored confidence. When the Barings failed in 1890, their house was taken over and alarm was checked by a show of strength which none felt inclined to doubt. The Reserve System was designed to perform a like service. It can now check and later mitigate the consequences of a boom which every prudent man knows must sometime collapse.

Unhappily, it is hampered by discounts made in aid of war bonds. Those discounts may however be segregated from the rest. Patriotic men who pledged their private resources to aid the government at a crisis should not be punished because traders who have become enormously rich have made a reckless use of their new-found wealth. Moreover, to force sales of government bonds is to impair the credit of the government and to put in question its good faith. The Reserve Association is a public institution. Men were asked to borrow in order to lend and induced to rely upon the credits granted to them. If in the effort to check imprudence now, meritorious creditors of the government be involved in ruin, the crisis will not be mitigated but aggravated. I can not think the men who control the reserve banks will be unequal to their responsibility.

Their power is immensely great. None can resist it.

That which should chiefly alarm us is the scarcity of capital the world over. Under other conditions, even of war, there are certain countries which at a pinch can afford some measure of help to one in distress. Today capital is scarce everywhere and no market can be found for securities or goods forced to sale by a pinch in the money market. The American panic of 1907 brought to us a flood of gold from England which eased the tension here. If today a crisis shall arise, no such relief can be got. Moreover, we ourselves are in such a situation that no class in the community can come to the rescue of any that shall need help. The securities market is glutted; credit is hard to get for any purpose. If by reason of strained credit forced sales of bonds and stocks become necessary, the prices of all securities must be dangerously depressed, and from that source it is altogether unlikely that adequate relief may be procured.

The recent action of the Reserve Board in raising the rate of discount has been too long delayed. Commitments have been entered upon which high rates of interest can not now undo. Goods and machinery must be purchased in advance. If the object of the increased rates is to gradually effect a deflation of the currency, falling prices are inevitable. A fall in prices will not only threaten the prosperity of traders but their credit. Yet deflation can not be avoided. The mischief involved in inflation is that it easily accomplishes a spurious prosperity which can not last. It is like drunkenness: first, elating, then depressing, then afflicting. The commercial world has been drunk and is still drunk. The longer the spree lasts, the greater its punishment. When it begins to sober up, its troubles will commence. High rates of interest are corrective, but the effect of the remedy must be to hasten the crisis.

Every nation is now on a paper basis. Not less than thirty billions of false money are in circulation. Such money has inflated not only the goods market but the credit market. To wring it out is to destroy the prosperity of traders and borrowers. Prices will fall; the values of securities will fall; the prosperity of all new enterprises will be checked; enlargements and betterments will be unprofitable; but the obligation of debts will be unaffected.

A quick remedy might be found in repudiation, but such a remedy would bring ruin. There are nations which will not pay $100 for what is worth $10. To pay $100 is to enrich the undeserving. If I have in my pocket marks which cost me 1 cent each, either in service or goods, I should not expect the State to pay me 25 cents, at the cost of other people who must be taxed to enrich me. No State has ever yet made such a sacrifice, even to preserve its credit.

No one can be certain of what will happen in the immediate future. Left alone, the business situation of today might be protracted for several years. Disturbed by despotic or benevolent measures, such as repudiation, deflation or enforced high rates for money, it may suddenly collapse. The safe course is a prudent one. Prudence may involve a loss of profits, but it can not result in bankruptcy.

We do not stand alone. We are a trading people, and a disturbance elsewhere can not fail to react here. If any country shall suddenly determine to reverse its policy and by violence to accomplish swiftly a rehabilitation of its currency, we must share in the ruin which will follow. No such

catastrophe is likely. Delay is
ever alluring. Procrastination
shifts the burden to other shoul-
ders, and men who perpetrate
blunders rarely have the courage
to confess their sins.

www.ingramcontent.com/pod-product-compliance
Lightning Source LLC
Chambersburg PA
CBHW030613270326
41927CB00007B/1151